The
Prayer
Map®

for Women

A Creative
Journal

BARBOUR
PUBLISHING

© 2018 by Barbour Publishing, Inc.

Simplicity ISBN 978-1-63609-762-6
Cherry Wildflowers ISBN 978-1-63609-763-3

Published by Barbour Publishing, Inc., 1810 Barbour Drive, Uhrichsville, Ohio 44683, www.barbourbooks.com

Our mission is to inspire the world with the life-changing message of the Bible.

 Member of the
Evangelical Christian
Publishers Association

Printed in China.

What Does Prayer Look Like?

Get ready to more fully experience the power of prayer in your everyday life with this creative journal. . .where every colorful page will guide you to create your very own prayer map—as you write out specific thoughts, ideas, and lists, which you can follow (from start to finish!)— as you talk to God. (Be sure to record the date on each one of your prayer maps so you can look back over time and see how God has continued to work in your life!) *The Prayer Map for Women* will not only encourage you to spend time talking with God about the things that matter most, it will also help you build a healthy spiritual habit of continual prayer for life!

Date:

Start Here

Dear Heavenly Father,..
....
....
....
....

Thank You for. . ...

I am worried about. . .

People I am praying for today. . .

›› Here's what's happening in my life. . . ..

....

....

....

.... ››

I need. . .

››

....

....   Other things on my heart that
                                  I need to share with You, God. . .
....

....

....

....

....

....

....

....

....

....

....

Amen.

**Thank You, Father,
for hearing my prayers.**

*"O Lord, please hear my prayer!
Listen to the prayers of those of us
who delight in honoring you."*
NEHEMIAH 1:11

Date:

Start Here

Dear Heavenly Father, ...
....
....
....
....

Thank You for. . . ....
....
....
....
....
....
....
....

People I am praying for today. . .
....
....
....
....
....
....

I am worried about. . .
....
....
....
....
....
....
....
....
....
....
....
....

Here's what's happening in my life. . . ..

....

....

....

....

I need. . .

....

....

....

....

....

....

....

....

....

....

....

....

Other things on my heart that
I need to share with You, God. . .

....

....

....

....

....

....

....

Amen.

**Thank You, Father,
for hearing my prayers.**

*The earnest prayer of a
righteous person has great power
and produces wonderful results.*
JAMES 5:16

Date:

Start Here

Dear Heavenly Father,...

....

....

....

....

Thank You for. . . ..

....

....

....

....

....

....

....

I am worried about...

....

....

....

....

....

....

....

....

....

People I am praying for today. . .

....

....

....

....

....

....

....

....

....

....

≫ Here's what's happening in my life. . . ....

....

....

....

.... ≫

I need. . .

....

....

....

....

....

....

....

....

....

....

....

....

....

≫

Other things on my heart that
I need to share with You, God. . .

....

....

....

....

....

....

....

Amen.

**Thank You, Father,
for hearing my prayers.**

*Listen to my cry for help,
my King and my God,
for I pray to no one but you.*
PSALM 5:2

Date:

Start Here

Dear Heavenly Father,

....

....

....

....

Thank You for. . .

....

....

....

....

....

....

....

I am worried about. . .

....

....

....

....

....

....

....

....

....

....

....

....

....

People I am praying for today. . .

....

....

....

....

....

....

⟫ Here's what's happening in my life. . . ..

....

....

....

.... **⟫**

I need. . .

⟫

....

....

....   Other things on my heart that
                                           I need to share with You, God. . .
....

....

....

....

....

....

....

....

....   *Amen.*

....   **Thank You, Father,
                                           for hearing my prayers.**

*Pray that the Lord's message
will spread rapidly and be
honored wherever it goes.*
2 Thessalonians 3:1

Date:

Start Here

Dear Heavenly Father, ...

....

....

....

....

Thank You for. . . ....

....

....

....

....

....

....

....

I am worried about. . .

....

....

....

....

....

....

....

....

....

....

....

People I am praying for today. . .

....

....

....

....

....

....

....

》》 Here's what's happening in my life. . . ..

....

....

....

.... **》》**

I need. . .

....

....

....

....

....

....

....

....

....

....

....

....

》》 Other things on my heart that
I need to share with You, God. . .

....

....

....

....

....

....

....

....

Amen.

**Thank You, Father,
for hearing my prayers.**

*"Keep on asking, and you will
receive what you ask for. Keep on seeking,
and you will find. Keep on knocking,
and the door will be opened to you."*
MATTHEW 7:7

Date:

Start Here

Dear Heavenly Father,

Thank You for. . .

I am worried about. . .

People I am praying for today. . .

⟫ Here's what's happening in my life. . .

I need. . .

⟫ Other things on my heart that I need to share with You, God. . .

♥♥
♥

Amen.

**Thank You, Father,
for hearing my prayers.**

*Hear me as I pray, O Lord.
Be merciful and answer me!*
PSALM 27:7

Date:

Start Here

Dear Heavenly Father, ...
....
....
....
....

Thank You for. . . ....
....
....
....
....
....
....
....

I am worried about. . .
....
....
....
....
....
....
....
....
....
....
....
....
....

People I am praying for today. . .
....
....
....
....
....
....
....

Here's what's happening in my life. . . ..

....

....

....

.... >>

I need. . .

....

....

....

....

....

....

....

....

....

....

....

....

Other things on my heart that
I need to share with You, God. . .

....

....

....

....

....

....

....

....

Amen.

**Thank You, Father,
for hearing my prayers.**

*Devote yourselves to prayer with an
alert mind and a thankful heart.*
COLOSSIANS 4:2

Date:

Start Here

Dear Heavenly Father, ...

....

....

....

....

Thank You for. . . ....

....

....

....

....

....

....

....

I am worried about. . .

....

....

....

....

....

....

....

....

People I am praying for today. . .

....

....

....

....

....

....

....

....

....

....

....

》》 Here's what's happening in my life. . .

....

....

....

....

....

》》

I need. . .

....

....

....

....

....

....

....

....

....

....

....

Other things on my heart that
I need to share with You, God. . .

....

....

....

....

....

....

....

Amen.

**Thank You, Father,
for hearing my prayers.**

*"O Lord, you are a great and awesome God!
You always fulfill your covenant and keep
your promises of unfailing love to those
who love you and obey your commands."*
Daniel 9:4

Date:

Start Here

Dear Heavenly Father,

Thank You for. . .

I am worried about. . .

People I am praying for today. . .

➤➤ Here's what's happening in my life. . . ..

....

....

....

....➤➤

I need. . .

....

....

....

....

....

....

....

....

....

....

....

....

➤➤

Other things on my heart that
I need to share with You, God. . .

....

....

....

....

....

....

....

Amen.

**Thank You, Father,
for hearing my prayers.**

*But each day the LORD pours his unfailing love
upon me, and through each night I sing his
songs, praying to God who gives me life.*
PSALM 42:8

Date: Start Here

Dear Heavenly Father, ...

....

....

....

....

Thank You for. . . ..

....

....

....

....

....

....

....

I am worried about. . .

....

....

....

....

....

....

....

....

People I am praying for today. . .

....

....

....

....

....

....

....

....

Here's what's happening in my life. . . ..

....
....
....
....

I need. . .

....
....
....
....
....
....
....
....
....
....
....
....
....

Other things on my heart that
I need to share with You, God. . .

....
....
....
....
....
....
....

Amen.

**Thank You, Father,
for hearing my prayers.**

*I pray that God, the source of hope,
will fill you completely with joy and
peace because you trust in him.*
ROMANS 15:13

Date:

Start Here

Dear Heavenly Father,..
....
....
....
....

Thank You for. . . ....

....

....

....

....

....

....

....

I am worried about. . .
....

....

....

....

....

....

....

....

....

....

....

People I am praying for today. . .
....

....

....

....

....

....

Here's what's happening in my life. . .

I need. . .

Other things on my heart that
I need to share with You, God. . .

Amen.
**Thank You, Father,
for hearing my prayers.**

*"Pray with all your might!
And don't let up!"*
1 SAMUEL 7:8 MSG

Date:

Start Here

Dear Heavenly Father, ...
....
....
....
....

Thank You for. . . ....
....
....
....
....
....
....
....

I am worried about. . .
....
....
....
....
....
....
....
....
....
....
....
....
....
....

People I am praying for today. . .
....
....
....
....
....
....
....

>> Here's what's happening in my life... ....

....

....

....

.... **>>**

I need...

....

....

....

....

....

....

....

....

....

....

....

....

....

....

>> Other things on my heart that
I need to share with You, God...

....

....

....

....

....

....

....

Amen.
**Thank You, Father,
for hearing my prayers.**

*We always pray for you,
and we give thanks to God,
the Father of our Lord Jesus Christ.*
COLOSSIANS 1:3

Date: _____

Start Here

Dear Heavenly Father, ...
....
....
....
....

Thank You for. . . ....
....
....
....
....
....
....
....

I am worried about. . .
....
....
....
....
....
....
....
....
....
....
....
....
....

People I am praying for today. . .
....
....
....
....
....
....

❯❯ Here's what's happening in my life. . .

....

....

....

....

❯❯

I need. . .

....

....

....

....

....

....

....

....

....

....

....

....

❯❯

Other things on my heart that
I need to share with You, God. . .

....

....

....

....

....

....

....

....

💜💙
💗
Amen.

**Thank You, Father,
for hearing my prayers.**

*Pray for all people.
Ask God to help them;
intercede on their behalf,
and give thanks for them.*
1 TIMOTHY 2:1

Date: _____ *Start Here*

Dear Heavenly Father, ...
....
....
....
....

Thank You for. . . ....

....
....
....
....
....
....

People I am praying for today. . .
....
....
....
....
....
....

I am worried about. . .
....
....
....
....
....
....
....
....
....
....
....
....
....

Here's what's happening in my life...

I need...

Other things on my heart that I need to share with You, God...

Amen.

Thank You, Father,
for hearing my prayers.

*Answer my prayers, O LORD,
for your unfailing love is wonderful.*
PSALM 69:16

Date: *Start Here*

Dear Heavenly Father, ...
....
....
....
....

Thank You for. . . ....

....

....

....

....

....

....

....

I am worried about. . .

....

....

....

....

....

....

....

....

....

....

....

....

....

People I am praying for today. . .

....

....

....

....

....

....

....

Here's what's happening in my life. . .

....

....

....

....

I need. . .

....

....

....

....

....

....

....

....

....

....

....

....

....

Other things on my heart that
I need to share with You, God. . .

....

....

....

....

....

....

....

....

Amen.

**Thank You, Father,
for hearing my prayers.**

*They will pray for you with deep
affection because of the overflowing
grace God has given to you.*
2 Corinthians 9:14

Date:

Start Here

Dear Heavenly Father, ...

....

....

....

....

Thank You for. . . ..

....

....

....

....

....

....

....

People I am praying for today. . .

....

....

....

....

....

....

I am worried about. . .

....

....

....

....

....

....

....

....

....

....

....

....

....

....

Here's what's happening in my life. . . ..

....

....

....

.... **»**

I need. . .

....

....

....

....

....

....

....

....

....

....

....

»

Other things on my heart that
I need to share with You, God. . .

....

....

....

....

....

....

....

Amen.

**Thank You, Father,
for hearing my prayers.**

*Because he bends down to listen,
I will pray as long as I have breath!*
PSALM 116:2

Date:

Start Here

Dear Heavenly Father, ...

....

....

....

....

Thank You for. . . ....

....

....

....

....

....

....

....

....

People I am praying for today. . .

....

....

....

....

....

....

....

I am worried about. . .

....

....

....

....

....

....

....

....

....

....

....

....

....

》》 Here's what's happening in my life. . . ..

....

....

....

....　**》》**

I need. . .

....

....　**》》**

....　　　Other things on my heart that
　　　　　　　　　　　　　　　I need to share with You, God. . .
....

....　　...

....　　...

....　　...

....　　...

....　　...

....　　...

....

....　　　　　　　　　*Amen.*

....　　　　**Thank You, Father,
　　　　　　　　　　　　　　for hearing my prayers.**

*I pray that from his glorious, unlimited
resources he will empower you with
inner strength through his Spirit.*
EPHESIANS 3:16

Date: _____

Start Here

Dear Heavenly Father, ...
....
....
....
....

Thank You for. . . ..
....
....
....
....
....
....
....

People I am praying for today. . .
....
....
....
....
....
....

I am worried about. . .
....
....
....
....
....
....
....
....
....
....
....
....
....

>> Here's what's happening in my life. . . ..

....

....

....

....

I need. . .

....

....

....

....

....

....

....

....

....

....

....

....

>> Other things on my heart that
I need to share with You, God. . .

....

....

....

....

....

....

....

Amen.

**Thank You, Father,
for hearing my prayers.**

GOD, O God of Israel, there is no God like
you in the skies above or on the earth below,
who unswervingly keeps covenant with his
servants and unfailingly loves them while they
sincerely live in obedience to your way.
2 CHRONICLES 6:14 MSG

Date:

Start Here

Dear Heavenly Father,...
....
....
....
....

Thank You for. . . ..
....
....
....
....
....
....
....
....

I am worried about. . .
....
....
....
....
....
....
....
....
....
....
....
....
....
....

People I am praying for today. . .
....
....
....
....
....
....
....

» **Here's what's happening in my life. . .** ....

....

....

....

.... **»**

I need. . .

....

....

....

....

....

....

....

....

....

....

....

....

»

Other things on my heart that
I need to share with You, God. . .

....

....

....

....

....

....

....

♥♥
♥
Amen.
**Thank You, Father,
for hearing my prayers.**

*God's way of putting people right shows up in
the acts of faith, confirming what Scripture has
said all along: "The person in right standing
before God by trusting him really lives."*
Romans 1:17 msg

«

Date:

Dear Heavenly Father, ...

....

....

....

....

Thank You for. . . ....

....

....

....

....

....

....

....

People I am praying for today. . .

....

....

....

....

....

....

....

I am worried about. . .

....

....

....

....

....

....

....

....

....

....

....

....

Here's what's happening in my life. . . ..

....

....

....

.... >>

I need. . .
....
....
....
....
....
....
....
....
....
....
....
....
....
....

Other things on my heart that
I need to share with You, God. . .

....

....

....

....

....

....

....

....

Amen.

Thank You, Father,
for hearing my prayers.

I lift my hands to you in prayer. I thirst for
you as parched land thirsts for rain.
PSALM 143:6

Date: Start Here

Dear Heavenly Father, ...
....
....
....
....

Thank You for. . . ....

....

....

....

....

....

....

....

People I am praying for today. . .

....

....

....

....

....

....

I am worried about. . .

....

....

....

....

....

....

....

....

....

....

....

....

....

....

» **Here's what's happening in my life. . .** ....

....

....

....

.... **»**

I need. . .

....

....

....

....

....

....

....

....

....

....

....

....

....

....

»

Other things on my heart that
I need to share with You, God. . .

....

....

....

....

....

....

....

....

....

Amen.

**Thank You, Father,
for hearing my prayers.**

*"Bless those who curse you.
Pray for those who hurt you."*
LUKE 6:28

Date:

Start Here

Dear Heavenly Father, ...

....

....

....

....

Thank You for. . . ..

....

....

....

....

....

....

....

I am worried about. . .

....

....

....

....

....

....

....

....

....

....

....

....

....

....

People I am praying for today. . .

....

....

....

....

....

....

Here's what's happening in my life. . .

....

....

....

....

I need. . .

....

....

....

....

....

....

....

....

....

....

....

Other things on my heart that
I need to share with You, God. . .

....

....

....

....

....

....

Amen.

**Thank You, Father,
for hearing my prayers.**

*I pray that your love will overflow more
and more, and that you will keep on growing
in knowledge and understanding.*
PHILIPPIANS 1:9

Date:

Start Here

Dear Heavenly Father, ...

....

....

....

....

Thank You for. . . ....

....

....

....

....

....

....

....

People I am praying for today. . .

....

....

....

....

....

....

I am worried about. . .

....

....

....

....

....

....

....

....

....

....

....

....

....

» Here's what's happening in my life. . .

....

....

....

.... **»**

I need. . .

....

....

....

....

....

....

....

....

....

....

....

....

....

»

Other things on my heart that
I need to share with You, God. . .

....

....

....

....

....

....

....

....

....

Amen.

Thank You, Father,
for hearing my prayers.

*"Love your enemies!
Pray for those who persecute you!"*
MATTHEW 5:44

Date:

Start Here

Dear Heavenly Father, ...
....
....
....
....

Thank You for. . . ....

....

....

....

....

....

....

....

People I am praying for today. . .

....

....

....

....

....

....

I am worried about. . .

....

....

....

....

....

....

....

....

....

....

....

....

....

》》 Here's what's happening in my life. . . ..

....

....

....

.... **》》**

I need. . .

....

....

....   **Other things on my heart that**
                             I need to share with You, God. . .
....

....

....

....

....

....

....

....

....   💜💜
                             💜
....   *Amen.*
                             Thank You, Father,
                             for hearing my prayers.

I'm thanking you, God, out loud in the streets,
singing your praises in town and country.
The deeper your love, the higher it goes;
every cloud is a flag to your faithfulness.
PSALM 57:9–10 MSG

Date:

Start Here

Dear Heavenly Father,

Thank You for. . .

I am worried about. . .

People I am praying for today. . .

》》 Here's what's happening in my life. . . ..

....

....

....

.... **》》**

I need. . .

》》

....

.... Other things on my heart that
I need to share with You, God. . .
....

....

....

....

....

....

....

....

....

.... Amen.

Thank You, Father,
for hearing my prayers.

I pray to you, O Lord, my rock.
PSALM 28:1

Date:

Start Here

Dear Heavenly Father, ...
....
....
....
....

Thank You for. . . ..
....
....
....
....
....
....
....
....

I am worried about. . .
....
....
....
....
....
....
....
....
....
....
....
....
....

People I am praying for today. . .
....
....
....
....
....
....
....

>> Here's what's happening in my life. . . ..

....

....

....

....   **>>**

I need. . .

....

....

....

....

....

....

....

....

....

....

....

....

....

Other things on my heart that
I need to share with You, God. . .

....

....

....

....

....

....

....

....

Amen.
**Thank You, Father,
for hearing my prayers.**

*I also pray that you will understand
the incredible greatness of God's
power for us who believe him.*
EPHESIANS 1:19

Date:

Start Here

Dear Heavenly Father,...

....

....

....

....

Thank You for. . ...

....

....

....

....

....

....

....

People I am praying for today. . .

....

....

....

....

....

....

I am worried about. . .

....

....

....

....

....

....

....

....

....

....

....

....

....

....

≫ Here's what's happening in my life. . . ..

....

....

....

....

≫

I need. . .

....

....

....

....

....

....

....

....

....

....

....

....

≫

Other things on my heart that
I need to share with You, God. . .

....

....

....

....

....

....

....

Amen.

**Thank You, Father,
for hearing my prayers.**

*"You can pray for anything, and if you
have faith, you will receive it."*
MATTHEW 21:22

Date:

Start Here

Dear Heavenly Father, ...
....
....
....
....

Thank You for. . . ....
....
....
....
....
....
....
....
....

I am worried about. . .
....
....
....
....
....
....
....
....
....
....
....
....
....

People I am praying for today. . .
....
....
....
....
....
....

Here's what's happening in my life. . . ..

....

....

....

....

I need. . .

....

....

....

....

....

....

....

....

....

....

....

....

....

Other things on my heart that
I need to share with You, God. . .

....

....

....

....

....

....

....

....

Amen.

**Thank You, Father,
for hearing my prayers.**

*In your unfailing love, O God, answer
my prayer with your sure salvation.*
PSALM 69:13

Date: _____

Start Here

Dear Heavenly Father, ...
....
....
....
....

Thank You for. . . ....
....
....
....
....
....
....
....

I am worried about. . .
....
....
....
....
....
....
....
....
....
....
....
....
....

People I am praying for today. . .
....
....
....
....
....
....
....

>> **Here's what's happening in my life. . .** ....

....

....

....

.... >>

I need. . .
....
....
....
....
....
....
....
....
....
....
....
....
....

>> Other things on my heart that
I need to share with You, God. . .

....

....

....

....

....

....

....

....

Amen.
**Thank You, Father,
for hearing my prayers.**

GOD, I'm telling the world what you do!
PSALM 73:28 MSG

Date:

Start Here

Dear Heavenly Father, ...
....
....
....
....

Thank You for. . . ....
....
....
....
....
....
....
....

I am worried about. . .
....
....
....
....
....
....
....
....
....
....
....
....
....
....

People I am praying for today. . .
....
....
....
....
....
....

>> **Here's what's happening in my life. . .** ....

....
....
....
.... >>

I need. . .

....
.... >>
....   Other things on my heart that
....   I need to share with You, God. . .
....
....
....
....
....
....
....
....
....
....

                                       ....

                                                                    ♥♥
                                                                     ♥
                                                                  Amen.
                                            **Thank You, Father,
                                          for hearing my prayers.**

*Jesus often withdrew to
the wilderness for prayer.*
LUKE 5:16

Date:

Dear Heavenly Father, ...
....
....
....
....

Thank You for. . . ..

....

....

....

....

....

....

....

People I am praying for today. . .

....

....

....

....

....

....

I am worried about. . .

....

....

....

....

....

....

....

....

....

....

....

....

>> Here's what's happening in my life. . . ..

....

....

....

....

I need. . .

....

....

....

....

....

....

....

....

....

....

....

....

....

Other things on my heart that
I need to share with You, God. . .

....

....

....

....

....

....

....

....

Amen.

**Thank You, Father,
for hearing my prayers.**

*Your love, GOD, is my song,
and I'll sing it! . . . I'll never quit
telling the story of your love.*
PSALM 89:1 MSG

Date:

Start Here

Dear Heavenly Father, ...
....
....
....
....

Thank You for. . . ..

I am worried about...

....

....

....

....

....

....

....

People I am praying for today. . .

....

....

....

....

....

》》 Here's what's happening in my life. . . ..

....

....

....

.... **》》**

I need. . .

....

....

....

....

....

....

....

....

....

....

....

Other things on my heart that
I need to share with You, God. . .

....

....

....

....

....

....

....

Amen.

**Thank You, Father,
for hearing my prayers.**

*Praise God, who did not
ignore my prayer or withdraw
his unfailing love from me.*
PSALM 66:20

Dear Heavenly Father, ...
....
....
....
....

Thank You for. . . ..

....

....

....

....

....

....

....

....

I am worried about. . .

....

....

....

....

....

....

....

....

....

....

....

....

People I am praying for today. . .

....

....

....

....

....

....

....

》》 Here's what's happening in my life. . . ..

....

....

....

....　》》

I need. . .

....

....

....

....

....

....

....

....

....

....

....

》》

Other things on my heart that
I need to share with You, God. . .

....

....

....

....

....

....

Amen.

**Thank You, Father,
for hearing my prayers.**

*The Holy Spirit prays for us
with groanings that cannot
be expressed in words.*
ROMANS 8:26

Date:

Start Here

Dear Heavenly Father,

....

....

....

....

Thank You for. . . ..

....

....

....

....

....

....

....

....

I am worried about. . .

....

....

....

....

....

....

....

....

....

....

....

....

People I am praying for today. . .

....

....

....

....

....

....

....

》》 Here's what's happening in my life. . . ..

....

....

....

.... **》》**

I need. . .

》》

....

.... Other things on my heart that

.... I need to share with You, God. . .

....

....

....

....

....

....

....

....

....

....

.... *Amen.*

Thank You, Father,
for hearing my prayers.

Rejoice in our confident hope.
Be patient in trouble,
and keep on praying.
ROMANS 12:12

《《

Date:

Start Here

Dear Heavenly Father,

Thank You for. . .

I am worried about. . .

People I am praying for today. . .

》 Here's what's happening in my life. . . ..

....
....
....
....》

I need. . .

》

Other things on my heart that
I need to share with You, God. . .

....
....
....
....
....
....

Amen.

**Thank You, Father,
for hearing my prayers.**

*I can't keep quiet about you.
GOD, my God, I can't thank you enough.*
PSALM 30:12 MSG

Date:

Start Here

Dear Heavenly Father, ...
....
....
....
....

Thank You for. . . ..

....

....

....

....

....

....

....

People I am praying for today. . .

....

....

....

....

....

....

I am worried about. . .

....

....

....

....

....

....

....

....

....

....

....

....

» **Here's what's happening in my life. . .** ....

....

....

....

.... **»**

I need. . .

....

....

....

....

....

....

....

....

....

....

....

....

....

»

Other things on my heart that
I need to share with You, God. . .

....

....

....

....

....

....

....

Amen.

**Thank You, Father,
for hearing my prayers.**

*I am praying to you because
I know you will answer, O God.
Bend down and listen as I pray.*
PSALM 17:6

Date: _____

Start Here

Dear Heavenly Father, ...
....
....
....
....

Thank You for. . . ....
....
....
....
....
....
....
....

I am worried about. . .
....
....
....
....
....
....
....
....
....
....
....
....

People I am praying for today. . .
....
....
....
....
....

Here's what's happening in my life. . . ..

....

....

....

....

I need. . .

....

....

....

....

....

....

....

....

....

....

....

....

Other things on my heart that
I need to share with You, God. . .

....

....

....

....

....

....

....

....

Amen.

**Thank You, Father,
for hearing my prayers.**

You are helping us by praying for us.
2 CORINTHIANS 1:11

Date:

Dear Heavenly Father, ...
....
....
....
....

Thank You for. . . ..
....
....
....
....
....
....
....

People I am praying for today. . .
....
....
....
....
....

I am worried about. . .
....
....
....
....
....
....
....
....
....
....
....
....
....

>> **Here's what's happening in my life. . .**

I need. . .

>>

Other things on my heart that
I need to share with You, God. . .

Amen.

**Thank You, Father,
for hearing my prayers.**

*I love the LORD because he hears my
voice and my prayer for mercy.*
PSALM 116:1

Date:

Start Here

Dear Heavenly Father, ...
....
....
....
....

Thank You for. . . ....

....

....

....

....

....

....

....

I am worried about. . .

....

....

....

....

....

....

....

....

....

....

....

....

People I am praying for today. . .

....

....

....

....

....

....

Here's what's happening in my life. . . ..

....

....

....

....

I need. . .
....
....
....
....
....
....
....
....
....
....
....
....
....

Other things on my heart that
I need to share with You, God. . .

....

....

....

....

....

....

Amen.

**Thank You, Father,
for hearing my prayers.**

*I have not stopped thanking God
for you. I pray for you constantly.*
EPHESIANS 1:16

Date:

Start Here

Dear Heavenly Father, ...
....
....
....
....

Thank You for. . . ..

....
....
....
....
....
....
....

I am worried about. . .

....
....
....
....
....
....
....
....
....
....
....
....

People I am praying for today. . .

....
....
....
....
....
....

Here's what's happening in my life. . .

I need. . .

Other things on my heart that
I need to share with You, God. . .

Amen.

**Thank You, Father,
for hearing my prayers.**

*The LORD is my strength and shield.
I trust him with all my heart. He helps
me, and my heart is filled with joy.
I burst out in songs of thanksgiving.*
PSALM 28:7

Start Here

Dear Heavenly Father, ...
....
....
....
....

Thank You for. . . ..
....
....
....
....
....
....
....
....

I am worried about. . .
....
....
....
....
....
....
....
....
....
....
....
....

People I am praying for today. . .
....
....
....
....
....
....

❯❯ Here's what's happening in my life. . .

I need. . .

Other things on my heart that
I need to share with You, God. . .

Amen.

Thank You, Father,
for hearing my prayers.

_I will praise you forever, O God,
for what you have done. I will
trust in your good name._
PSALM 52:9

Date:

Dear Heavenly Father, ...

....

....

....

....

Thank You for. . . ..

....

....

....

....

....

....

....

People I am praying for today. . .

....

....

....

....

....

....

I am worried about. . .

....

....

....

....

....

....

....

....

....

....

....

....

....

》 Here's what's happening in my life. . . ..

....
....
....
....

I need. . .

....
....
....
....
....
....
....
....
....
....
....
....

Other things on my heart that
I need to share with You, God. . .

....
....
....
....
....
....
....

Amen.

**Thank You, Father,
for hearing my prayers.**

*You faithfully answer our prayers
with awesome deeds, O God our savior.
You are the hope of everyone on earth,
even those who sail on distant seas.*
PSALM 65:5

Date: *Start Here*

Dear Heavenly Father,..
....
....
....
....

Thank You for. . ...
....
....
....
....
....
....
....

I am worried about...
....
....
....
....
....
....
....
....
....
....
....
....

People I am praying for today. . .
....
....
....
....
....
....

≫ Here's what's happening in my life. . .

I need. . .

≫

Other things on my heart that
I need to share with You, God. . .

Amen.
**Thank You, Father,
for hearing my prayers.**

*Pray in the Spirit at all times and on every
occasion. Stay alert and be persistent in
your prayers for all believers everywhere.*
Ephesians 6:18

Date:

Start Here

Dear Heavenly Father, ...
....
....
....
....

Thank You for. . . ..
....
....
....
....
....
....
....

People I am praying for today. . .
....
....
....
....
....
....

I am worried about. . .
....
....
....
....
....
....
....
....
....
....
....
....
....
....

» **Here's what's happening in my life. . .** ....

....

....

....

.... **»**

I need. . .

....

....

....

....

....

....

....

....

....

....

....

Other things on my heart that
I need to share with You, God. . .

....

....

....

....

....

....

Amen.

**Thank You, Father,
for hearing my prayers.**

O Lord of Heaven's Armies,
what joy for those who trust in you.
Psalm 84:12

Start Here

Dear Heavenly Father, ...
....
....
....
....

Thank You for. . . ..
....
....
....
....
....
....
....

People I am praying for today. . .
....
....
....
....
....
....

I am worried about. . .
....
....
....
....
....
....
....
....
....
....
....
....

Here's what's happening in my life. . . ..

....

....

....

.... >>

I need. . .

....

....

....

....

....

....

....

....

....

....

....

....

....

Other things on my heart that
I need to share with You, God. . .

....

....

....

....

....

....

....

Amen.

**Thank You, Father,
for hearing my prayers.**

*Whenever I pray,
I make my requests. . .with joy.*
PHILIPPIANS 1:4

Date:

Dear Heavenly Father,..

....

....

....

....

Thank You for. . . ..

....

....

....

....

....

....

....

I am worried about. . .

....

....

....

....

....

....

....

....

....

....

People I am praying for today. . .

....

....

....

....

....

....

Here's what's happening in my life. . . ..

....

....

....

....

I need. . .

....

....

....

....

....

....

....

....

....

....

....

....

....

Other things on my heart that
I need to share with You, God. . .

....

....

....

....

....

....

....

Amen.

**Thank You, Father,
for hearing my prayers.**

"When you are praying, first forgive anyone
you are holding a grudge against, so that your
Father in heaven will forgive your sins, too."
MARK 11:25

Date: _Start Here_

📍 **Dear Heavenly Father,** ....
....
....
....
....

🧭

Thank You for. . . ....
....
....
....
....
....
....
....

People I am praying for today. . .
....
....
....
....
....
....

I am worried about. . .
....
....
....
....
....
....
....
....
....
....
....

Here's what's happening in my life. . .

I need. . .

Other things on my heart that
I need to share with You, God. . .

Amen.

**Thank You, Father,
for hearing my prayers.**

*Don't worry about anything; instead,
pray about everything. Tell God what you
need, and thank him for all he has done.*
PHILIPPIANS 4:6

Start Here

Dear Heavenly Father, ...

....

....

....

....

Thank You for. . . ..

I am worried about...

People I am praying for today. . .

>> Here's what's happening in my life. . . ..

....
....
....
.... **>>**

I need. . .
....
....
....
.... **>>**
....   Other things on my heart that
....   I need to share with You, God. . .
....
....
....
....
....
....
....
....
....

Amen.

**Thank You, Father,
for hearing my prayers.**

*I am praying that you will put into action
the generosity that comes from your faith
as you understand and experience all
the good things we have in Christ.*

PHILEMON 1:6

Date:

Start Here

Dear Heavenly Father,..

....

....

....

....

Thank You for. . ...

....

....

....

....

....

....

....

I am worried about. . .

....

....

....

....

....

....

....

....

....

....

....

People I am praying for today. . .

....

....

....

....

....

....

....

» **Here's what's happening in my life. . .** ....

....

....

....

.... **»**

I need. . .

....

....

....

....

....

....

....

....

....

....

....

....

» Other things on my heart that
I need to share with You, God. . .

....

....

....

....

....

....

....

Amen.

**Thank You, Father,
for hearing my prayers.**

*We have not stopped praying for you since
we first heard about you. We ask God to give
you complete knowledge of his will and to
give you spiritual wisdom and understanding.*
COLOSSIANS 1:9

Dear Heavenly Father, ...
....
....
....
....

Thank You for. . . ..

....

....

....

....

....

....

....

....

People I am praying for today. . .

....

....

....

....

....

....

I am worried about...

....

....

....

....

....

....

....

....

....

....

....

....

....

....

»» Here's what's happening in my life. . . ..

....

....

....

.... »»

I need. . .

....

....

....

....

....

....

....

....

....

....

....

....

»»

Other things on my heart that
I need to share with You, God. . .

....

....

....

....

....

....

....

Amen.

**Thank You, Father,
for hearing my prayers.**

*I will praise you as long as I live,
lifting up my hands to you in prayer.*
PSALM 63:4

Date: _____ *Start Here*

📍 **Dear Heavenly Father,** ....
....
....
....
....

Thank You for. . . ....

....

....   **I am worried about. . .**

....

....

....

....

....

....

....

People I am praying for today. . .   ....

....

....

....

....

....

....

....

Here's what's happening in my life. . .

I need. . .

Other things on my heart that
I need to share with You, God. . .

Amen.

**Thank You, Father,
for hearing my prayers.**

*"Pray like this: Our Father in heaven,
may your name be kept holy."*
MATTHEW 6:9

Date:

Start Here

Dear Heavenly Father, ...
....
....
....
....

Thank You for. . . ....
....
....
....
....
....
....
....

I am worried about. . .
....
....
....
....
....
....
....
....
....
....
....
....

People I am praying for today. . .
....
....
....
....
....
....

》》 Here's what's happening in my life. . .

I need. . .

Other things on my heart that
I need to share with You, God. . .

Amen.
**Thank You, Father,
for hearing my prayers.**

*We keep on praying for you, asking our God
to enable you to live a life worthy of his call.*
2 Thessalonians 1:11

Date: _____

Start Here

Dear Heavenly Father, ...

....

....

....

....

Thank You for. . . ....

....

....

....

....

....

....

....

I am worried about. . .

....

....

....

....

....

....

....

....

....

....

....

....

....

....

People I am praying for today. . .

....

....

....

....

....

....

≫ Here's what's happening in my life. . .

....

....

....

....

I need. . .

....

....

....

....

....

....

....

....

....

....

....

Other things on my heart that
I need to share with You, God. . .

....

....

....

....

....

....

Amen.

**Thank You, Father,
for hearing my prayers.**

*As soon as I pray, you answer me;
you encourage me by giving me strength.*
PSALM 138:3

Date:

Start Here

Dear Heavenly Father,

Thank You for. . .

People I am praying for today. . .

I am worried about. . .

≫ Here's what's happening in my life. . .

I need. . .

≫ Other things on my heart that
I need to share with You, God. . .

Amen.

Thank You, Father,
for hearing my prayers.

*Trust in the Lord with all your heart;
do not depend on your own understanding.*
Proverbs 3:5

Date:

Start Here

Dear Heavenly Father,
....
....
....
....
....

Thank You for. . . ....
....
....
....
....
....
....
....

People I am praying for today. . .
....
....
....
....
....
....

I am worried about. . .
....
....
....
....
....
....
....
....
....
....
....
....
....
....

Here's what's happening in my life. . .

I need. . .

Other things on my heart that
I need to share with You, God. . .

Amen.

**Thank You, Father,
for hearing my prayers.**

*I prayed to the LORD, and he answered
me. He freed me from all my fears.*
PSALM 34:4

Start Here

Dear Heavenly Father, ...

....

....

....

....

Thank You for. . . ..

....

....

....

....

....

....

....

I am worried about. . .

....

....

....

....

....

....

....

....

....

....

....

....

....

....

People I am praying for today. . .

....

....

....

....

....

....

Here's what's happening in my life. . . ..

....

....

....

.... »

I need. . .

....

....

....

....

....

....

....

....

....

....

....

....

Other things on my heart that
I need to share with You, God. . .

....

....

....

....

....

....

....

....

....

Amen.

**Thank You, Father,
for hearing my prayers.**

*In every place of worship, I want men to
pray with holy hands lifted up to God,
free from anger and controversy.*
1 TIMOTHY 2:8

Date:

Start Here

Dear Heavenly Father, ...
....
....
....
....

Thank You for. . . ..
....
....
....
....
....
....
....

People I am praying for today. . .
....
....
....
....
....
....

I am worried about. . .
....
....
....
....
....
....
....
....
....
....
....
....
....

》》 Here's what's happening in my life. . . ..

....

....

....

.... **》》**

I need. . .

》》

....

....

....

....

....

....

....

....

....

....

....

....

....

Other things on my heart that
I need to share with You, God. . .

....

....

....

....

....

....

Amen.

**Thank You, Father,
for hearing my prayers.**

*"I tell you, you can pray for anything,
and if you believe that you've
received it, it will be yours."*
MARK 11:24

Date:

Start Here

Dear Heavenly Father, ...
....
....
....
....

Thank You for. . . ..

I am worried about. . .

People I am praying for today. . .

Here's what's happening in my life. . .

....
....
....
....

I need. . .

....
....
....
....
....
....
....
....
....
....
....
....

Other things on my heart that
I need to share with You, God. . .

....
....
....
....
....
....

Amen.

**Thank You, Father,
for hearing my prayers.**

*Are any of you suffering hardships?
You should pray. Are any of you
happy? You should sing praises.*
JAMES 5:13

Date:

Dear Heavenly Father, ...

....

....

....

....

Thank You for. . . ..

....

....

....

....

....

....

....

I am worried about. . .

....

....

....

....

....

....

....

....

....

....

....

....

People I am praying for today. . .

....

....

....

....

....

....

>> Here's what's happening in my life. . .

I need. . .

>> Other things on my heart that
I need to share with You, God. . .

♥♥
♥
Amen.

**Thank You, Father,
for hearing my prayers.**

*I pray to you, O LORD. I say,
"You are my place of refuge.
You are all I really want in life."*
PSALM 142:5

Date:

Start Here

Dear Heavenly Father, ...

....

....

....

....

Thank You for. . . ..

....

....

....

....

....

....

....

I am worried about. . .

....

....

....

....

....

....

....

....

....

....

....

....

People I am praying for today. . .

....

....

....

....

....

....

》》 Here's what's happening in my life. . . ..

....

....

....

.... **》》**

I need. . .

....

....

....

....

....

....

....

....

....

....

....

....

》》 Other things on my heart that
I need to share with You, God. . .

....

....

....

....

....

....

Amen.

**Thank You, Father,
for hearing my prayers.**

*Remember that the heavenly Father to
whom you pray has no favorites.*
1 PETER 1:17

Date:

Start Here

Dear Heavenly Father,...
....
....
....
....

Thank You for. . ...

....

....

....

....

....

....

....

I am worried about. . .

....

....

....

....

....

....

People I am praying for today. . .

....

....

....

....

....

....

....

....

....

....

Here's what's happening in my life. . . ..

....

....

....

....

I need. . .

....

....

....

....

....

....

....

....

....

....

....

....

Other things on my heart that
I need to share with You, God. . .

....

....

....

....

....

....

....

....

Amen.

**Thank You, Father,
for hearing my prayers.**

*If we are faithful to the end, trusting
God just as firmly as when we first believed,
we will share in all that belongs to Christ.*
HEBREWS 3:14

Date:

Start Here

Dear Heavenly Father, ...

....

....

....

....

Thank You for. . . ....

....

....

....

....

....

....

....

People I am praying for today. . .

....

....

....

....

....

....

I am worried about. . .

....

....

....

....

....

....

....

....

....

....

....

....

Here's what's happening in my life. . .

I need. . .

Other things on my heart that
I need to share with You, God. . .

Amen.
Thank You, Father,
for hearing my prayers.

*The Lord. . .delights in the
prayers of the upright.*
PROVERBS 15:8

Date:

Start Here

Dear Heavenly Father, ...
....
....
....
....

Thank You for. . . ..
....
....
....
....
....
....
....

I am worried about. . .
....
....
....
....
....
....
....
....
....
....
....
....

People I am praying for today. . .
....
....
....
....
....
....

Here's what's happening in my life... ....

....
....
....
....

I need. . .

....
....
....
....
....
....
....
....
....
....
....
....

Other things on my heart that
I need to share with You, God. . .

....
....
....
....
....
....
....
....

Amen.

**Thank You, Father,
for hearing my prayers.**

*But you, dear friends, must build each
other up in your most holy faith,
pray in the power of the Holy Spirit.*
JUDE 1:20

Date:

Start Here

Dear Heavenly Father, ...

....

....

....

....

Thank You for. . . ..

....

....

....

....

....

....

....

I am worried about. . .

....

....

....

....

....

....

....

....

....

....

....

People I am praying for today. . .

....

....

....

....

....

....

》》 Here's what's happening in my life. . . ..

....
....
....

.... **》》**

I need. . .

》》

Other things on my heart that
I need to share with You, God. . .

....
....
....
....
....
....
....

Amen.

**Thank You, Father,
for hearing my prayers.**

*Bless those who persecute you.
Don't curse them; pray that
God will bless them.*
ROMANS 12:14

Date: _Start Here_

Dear Heavenly Father, ...
....
....
....
....

Thank You for. . . ..

....

....

....

....

....

....

....

People I am praying for today. . .

....

....

....

....

....

....

I am worried about. . .

....

....

....

....

....

....

....

....

....

....

....

....

....

....

➤➤ Here's what's happening in my life. . . ..

....

....

....

.... ➤➤

I need. . .

....

....

....

....

....

....

....

....

....

....

....

....

....

Other things on my heart that
I need to share with You, God. . .

....

....

....

....

....

....

....

....

Amen.

**Thank You, Father,
for hearing my prayers.**

The LORD will answer my prayer.
PSALM 6:9

Date: _____

Start Here

Dear Heavenly Father, ...
....
....
....
....

Thank You for. . . ....
....
....
....
....
....
....
....
....

People I am praying for today. . .
....
....
....
....
....
....

I am worried about. . .
....
....
....
....
....
....
....
....
....
....
....
....

>> Here's what's happening in my life. . . ..

....

....

....

.... **>>**

I need. . .

....

....

....

....

....

....

....

....

....

....

....

....

>>

Other things on my heart that
I need to share with You, God. . .

....

....

....

....

....

....

....

....

Amen.

**Thank You, Father,
for hearing my prayers.**

God can be trusted to keep his promise.
HEBREWS 10:23

Date:

Start Here

Dear Heavenly Father,...
....
....
....
....

Thank You for. . . ....

....

....

....

....

....

....

....

I am worried about. . .

....

....

....

....

....

....

....

....

....

....

....

....

....

People I am praying for today. . .

....

....

....

....

....

....

Here's what's happening in my life. . . ..

....

....

....

....

.... **》》**

I need. . .

....

....

....

....

....

....

....

....

....

....

....

....

Other things on my heart that
I need to share with You, God. . .

....

....

....

....

....

....

....

....

Amen.

**Thank You, Father,
for hearing my prayers.**

*But I'm in the very presence of GOD—
oh, how refreshing it is!*
PSALM 73:27 MSG

Date:

Start Here

Dear Heavenly Father, ...
....
....
....
....

Thank You for. . . ..

....

....

....

....

....

....

....

I am worried about. . .

....

....

....

....

....

....

....

....

....

....

....

....

....

People I am praying for today. . .

....

....

....

....

....

....

➤➤ Here's what's happening in my life. . . ..

....

....

....

.... ➤➤

I need. . .

....

....

....

....

....

....

....

....

....

....

....

....

....

Other things on my heart that
I need to share with You, God. . .

....

....

....

....

....

....

....

♥♥
♥
Amen.
**Thank You, Father,
for hearing my prayers.**

*Let your unfailing love surround us,
LORD, for our hope is in you alone.*
PSALM 33:22

Date:

Dear Heavenly Father, ...

....

....

....

....

Thank You for. . . ..

....

....

....

....

....

....

....

....

I am worried about. . .

....

....

....

....

....

....

....

....

....

People I am praying for today. . .

....

....

....

....

....

....

....

》》 Here's what's happening in my life. . . ..

....

....

....

.... 》》

I need. . .

....

....

.... 》》

....   Other things on my heart that

....   I need to share with You, God. . .

....

....

....

....

....

....

....

....

Amen.

**Thank You, Father,
for hearing my prayers.**

*Pray. . .for kings and all who are in authority
so that we can live peaceful and quiet
lives marked by godliness and dignity.*
1 TIMOTHY 2:2

Date:

Dear Heavenly Father,..
....
....
....
....

Thank You for. . ...

....

....

....

....

....

....

....

I am worried about. . .

....

....

....

....

....

....

....

....

....

....

....

....

....

People I am praying for today. . .

....

....

....

....

....

....

»» Here's what's happening in my life. . . ..

....

....

....

.... **»»**

I need. . .

....

.... **»»**

....   Other things on my heart that
                                   I need to share with You, God. . .
....

....

....

....

....

....

....

....

....

....   *Amen.*

                             Thank You, Father,
                             for hearing my prayers.

O Lord, you alone are my hope.
PSALM 71:5

Date:

Dear Heavenly Father, ...
....
....
....
....

Thank You for. . . ..
....
....
....
....
....
....
....
....

I am worried about. . .
....
....
....
....
....
....
....
....
....
....
....
....
....
....

People I am praying for today. . .
....
....
....
....
....
....
....

Here's what's happening in my life. . .

I need. . .

Other things on my heart that
I need to share with You, God. . .

Amen.

**Thank You, Father,
for hearing my prayers.**

*"The eyes of the Lord watch over
those who do right, and his ears
are open to their prayers."*
1 Peter 3:12

Date:

Dear Heavenly Father, ...

....

....

....

....

Thank You for... ....

....

....

....

....

....

....

....

I am worried about...

....

....

....

....

....

....

....

....

....

....

....

....

People I am praying for today...

....

....

....

....

....

....

» Here's what's happening in my life. . . ..
....
....
....
.... **»**

I need. . .

....

....

....

....

....

....

....

....

....

....

....

....

....

» Other things on my heart that
I need to share with You, God. . .

....

....

....

....

....

....

....

....

Amen.

**Thank You, Father,
for hearing my prayers.**

*"But when you pray, go away by yourself,
shut the door behind you, and pray to your
Father in private. Then your Father,
who sees everything, will reward you."*
MATTHEW 6:6

Date: _Start Here_

📍 **Dear Heavenly Father,** ....
....
....
....
....

Thank You for... ....
....
....
....
....
....
....
....

I am worried about...
....
....
....
....
....
....
....
....
....
....
....
....

People I am praying for today...
....
....
....
....
....
....
....

>> Here's what's happening in my life. . . ..

....

....

....

.... **>>**

I need. . .

>>

Other things on my heart that
I need to share with You, God. . .

....

....

....

....

....

....

....

....

....

....

....

....

....

Amen.

Thank You, Father,
for hearing my prayers.

Be earnest and disciplined in your prayers.
1 Peter 4:7

Date:

Start Here

Dear Heavenly Father, ...
....
....
....
....

Thank You for. . . ..
....
....
....
....
....
....
....

I am worried about. . .
....
....
....
....
....
....
....
....
....
....
....
....
....

People I am praying for today. . .
....
....
....
....
....
....

>> Here's what's happening in my life... ....

....

....

....

.... >>

I need...

....

....

....

....

....

....

....

....

....

....

....

>> Other things on my heart that
I need to share with You, God...

....

....

....

....

....

....

....

....

Amen.

**Thank You, Father,
for hearing my prayers.**

*Hallelujah! O my soul, praise GOD!
All my life long I'll praise GOD, singing
songs to my God as long as I live.*
PSALM 146:1–2 MSG

Date:

Start Here

Dear Heavenly Father, ...
....
....
....
....

Thank You for. . . ....

....

....

....

....

....

....

....

People I am praying for today. . .

....

....

....

....

....

....

I am worried about. . .

....

....

....

....

....

....

....

....

....

....

....

....

Here's what's happening in my life. . . ..

....

....

....

....

I need. . .

....

....

....

....

....

....

....

....

....

....

....

....

Other things on my heart that
I need to share with You, God. . .

....

....

....

....

....

....

....

....

Amen.

**Thank You, Father,
for hearing my prayers.**

*When doubts filled my mind, your comfort
gave me renewed hope and cheer.*
PSALM 94:19

Date:

Start Here

Dear Heavenly Father,..
....
....
....
....

Thank You for. . ...
....
....
....
....
....
....
....

People I am praying for today. . .
....
....
....
....
....
....

I am worried about. . .
....
....
....
....
....
....
....
....
....
....
....
....
....

Here's what's happening in my life. . .

....

....

....

....

I need. . .

....

....

....

....

....

....

....

....

....

....

....

....

....

....

Other things on my heart that
I need to share with You, God. . .

....

....

....

....

....

....

....

Amen.

**Thank You, Father,
for hearing my prayers.**

*I am counting on the LORD;
yes, I am counting on him.*
PSALM 130:5

Date:

📍 **Dear Heavenly Father,**...
....
....
....
....

Thank You for. . . ....

....

....

....

....

....

....

....

People I am praying for today. . .

....

....

....

....

....

....

....

I am worried about. . .

....

....

....

....

....

....

....

....

....

....

....

....

» **Here's what's happening in my life. . .** ....

....

....

....

.... **»**

I need. . .

....

....

....

....

....

....

....

....

....

....

....

....

....

» Other things on my heart that
I need to share with You, God. . .

....

....

....

....

....

....

....

Amen.

**Thank You, Father,
for hearing my prayers.**

*"No one who trusts God like this—
heart and soul—will ever regret it."*
ROMANS 10:11 MSG

Date:

Start Here

Dear Heavenly Father, ...
....
....
....
....

Thank You for. . . ....

| I am worried about... |

....

....

....

....

....

....

....

People I am praying for today. . .

....

....

....

....

....

....

Here's what's happening in my life. . . ..

....

....

....

....

I need. . .

....

....

....

Other things on my heart that
I need to share with You, God. . .

....

....

....

....

....

....

....

....

....

....

....

....

....

....

....

....

....

Amen.

**Thank You, Father,
for hearing my prayers.**

*The hopes of the godly
result in happiness.*
PROVERBS 10:28

Date:

Start Here

Dear Heavenly Father, ...
....
....
....
....

Thank You for. . . ..

....

....

....

....

....

....

....

I am worried about. . .

....

....

....

....

....

....

....

....

....

....

....

People I am praying for today. . .

....

....

....

....

....

....

Here's what's happening in my life. . .

....
....
....
....

I need. . .

....
....
....
....
....
....
....
....
....
....
....
....

Other things on my heart that
I need to share with You, God. . .

....
....
....
....
....
....
....

Amen.

**Thank You, Father,
for hearing my prayers.**

*God knows how often I pray for you.
Day and night I bring you and your needs in
prayer to God, whom I serve with all my heart
by spreading the Good News about his Son.*
ROMANS 1:9

Date:

Start Here

Dear Heavenly Father, ...

....

....

....

....

Thank You for. . . ....

....

....

....

....

....

....

....

I am worried about. . .

....

....

....

....

....

....

....

....

....

....

....

....

....

....

People I am praying for today. . .

....

....

....

....

....

....

❯❯ Here's what's happening in my life. . .

. . . .

. . . .

. . . .

. . . . ❯❯

I need. . .

Other things on my heart that
I need to share with You, God. . .

Amen.

**Thank You, Father,
for hearing my prayers.**

*You're my place of quiet retreat;
I wait for your Word to renew me.*
PSALM 119:113 MSG

Date: _____

Start Here

Dear Heavenly Father,..
....
....
....
....

Thank You for. . ...
....
....
....
....
....
....
....

People I am praying for today. . .
....
....
....
....
....

I am worried about. . .
....
....
....
....
....
....
....
....
....
....
....

>> Here's what's happening in my life. . . ..

....

....

....

.... >>

I need. . .

....

....   Other things on my heart that
                                                     I need to share with You, God. . .
....

....

....

....

....

....

....

....

....

....   💜💜💜

....   *Amen.*

....   **Thank You, Father,
                                                         for hearing my prayers.**

*Quiet down before God,
be prayerful before him.*
PSALM 37:7 MSG

Date:

Start Here

Dear Heavenly Father,

Thank You for. . .

I am worried about. . .

People I am praying for today. . .

Here's what's happening in my life. . .

I need. . .

Other things on my heart that
I need to share with You, God. . .

Amen.

Thank You, Father,
for hearing my prayers.

*I thank you for answering my
prayer and giving me victory!*
PSALM 118:21

Date:

Start Here

Dear Heavenly Father, ...

....

....

....

....

Thank You for. . . ....

....

....

....

....

....

....

....

People I am praying for today. . .

....

....

....

....

....

....

I am worried about. . .

....

....

....

....

....

....

....

....

....

....

....

....

》》 Here's what's happening in my life. . . ..

....

....

....

.... 》》

I need. . .

....

....

....

....

....

....

....

....

....

....

....

....

....

》》

Other things on my heart that
I need to share with You, God. . .

....

....

....

....

....

....

....

....

Amen.

**Thank You, Father,
for hearing my prayers.**

*I pray that your hearts will be flooded with
light so that you can understand the confident
hope he has given to those he called.*
EPHESIANS 1:18

Date:

Start Here

Dear Heavenly Father, ...
....
....
....
....

Thank You for. . . ..
....
....
....
....
....
....
....

People I am praying for today. . .
....
....
....
....
....
....

I am worried about. . .
....
....
....
....
....
....
....
....
....
....
....
....

I need. . .

Other things on my heart that
I need to share with You, God. . .

Amen.

**Thank You, Father,
for hearing my prayers.**

Answer me when I call to you, O God.
PSALM 4:1

Date: .... *Start Here* - - - - -

Dear Heavenly Father, ...
....
....
....
....

Thank You for. . . ....

....
....   **I am worried about. . .**
....
....
....
....
....
....
....
                                                                  ....
People I am praying for today. . .   ....
....
....
....
....
....
....

Here's what's happening in my life. . . ..

....
....
....
....

I need. . .

....
....
....
....
....
....
....
....
....
....
....
....
....
....

Other things on my heart that
I need to share with You, God. . .

....
....
....
....
....
....
....
....

Amen.

**Thank You, Father,
for hearing my prayers.**

*Every time I think of you,
I give thanks to my God.*
PHILIPPIANS 1:3

Date: *Start Here*

Dear Heavenly Father, ...
....
....
....
....

Thank You for. . . ....
....
....
....
....
....
....
....

I am worried about. . .
....
....
....
....
....
....
....
....
....
....
....
....
....

People I am praying for today. . .
....
....
....
....
....
....

Here's what's happening in my life. . .

I need. . .

Other things on my heart that
I need to share with You, God. . .

Amen.

**Thank You, Father,
for hearing my prayers.**

Never stop praying.
1 Thessalonians 5:17

CHECK OUT THESE FAITH MAPS FOR THE ENTIRE FAMILY...

The Prayer Map for Men
978-1-64352-438-2

The Prayer Map for Women
978-1-63609-762-2/
978-1-63609-763-3

The Prayer Map for Girls
978-1-68322-559-1

The Prayer Map for Boys
978-1-68322-558-4

The Prayer Map for Teens
978-1-68322-556-0

These purposeful prayer journals are a fun and creative way to more fully experience the power of prayer. Each page guides you to write out thoughts, ideas, and lists. . .creating a specific "map" for you to follow as you talk to God. Each map includes a spot to record the date, so you can look back on your prayers and see how God has worked in your life. *The Prayer Map* will not only encourage you to spend time talking with God about the things that matter most. . .it will also help you build a healthy spiritual habit of continual prayer for life!

Spiral Bound